D1360839

INSTACRAFT

Fun & Simple Projects for Adorable Gifts, Décor & More

By Alison Caporimo

Photography by Meera Lee Patel

Ulysses Press

Text copyright © 2013 Alison Caporimo. Photographs and illustrations copyright © 2013 Meera Lee Patel. Design and concept © 2013 Ulysses Press and its licensors. All rights reserved. No part of this publication may be reproduced, stored in a retrieval system, or transmitted in any form or by any means without the prior written permission of the publisher, nor be otherwise circulated in any form of binding or cover other than that in which it is published and without a similar condition being imposed on the subsequent purchaser.

Published in the U.S. by
Ulysses Press
P.O. Box 3440
Berkeley, CA 94703
www.ulyssespress.com

ISBN: 978-1-61243-236-6
Library of Congress Control Number 2013938283

Printed in the United States by Bang Printing

10 9 8 7 6 5 4 3 2 1

Acquisitions Editor: Katherine Furman
Managing Editor: Claire Chun
Editor: Melanie Gold
Proofreader: Elyce Berrigan-Dunlop
Design and layout: Elliot Stokes
Indexer: Jay Kreider

Distributed by Publishers Group West

IMPORTANT NOTE TO READERS: This book is independently authored and published and no sponsorship or endorsement of this book by, and no affiliation with, any celebrities, trademarked brands or other products mentioned or pictured within is claimed or suggested. All trademarks that appear in directions, photographs, and elsewhere in this book belong to their respective owners and are used here for informational purposes only. The author and publisher encourage readers to patronize the quality brands and products mentioned and pictured in this book.

FOR MY FAMILY

CONTENTS

HELLO THERE!

Not long ago we used to chop and chisel instead of swipe and tap. We carved and constructed. Why, we even whittled. While our processes have changed, it's still a fact: we love to do things with our hands. That is why I spent the better part of a year sitting at a paint-dashed desk creating and testing various simple crafts—so you can sit down and make something special in no time at all.

This book is an invitation to remember our roots, but it also invites us to revise them. I will not ask you to chop or carve, but I will encourage you to spray and hang, cut and fold, and maybe even dip. There will be paint and there will be scissors and maybe a few more grade-school basics, but most of all there will be fun—with the added bonus of simple handmade projects you can share.

As for my shopping list, I included nothing that you won't find lying around the house or in the recycling bin (glass bottles, take-out containers, and even Tic Tac dispensers have all made it into this book). If you're going to venture out for a material or two, the only place you need to look is in a local hardware store. While you're there, pick up some E-6000 glue, which is my preference when it comes to strong crafting glues.

When you do sit down to craft, give a listen to the song suggestions I've made while you spray-paint, try out a recipe during a project's dry time, or use a special tip for a variation on your favorite creation. I've woven these extras throughout the following pages to keep you creating even while you're creating.

This book is for everyone: those who are plugged in and logged on, and those like my grandmother who couldn't touch the seam of a single dress without naming its stitch. Whether you feel like you don't have time to craft or were born without an artistic bone in your body or simply haven't gotten around to trying it yet, this book was made with you in mind, with the hopes that you'll make something new rather than buy it or rethink a box or bottle before tossing it. These wishes I pass from me to you, from my hands to yours.

Now, let's make something beautiful.

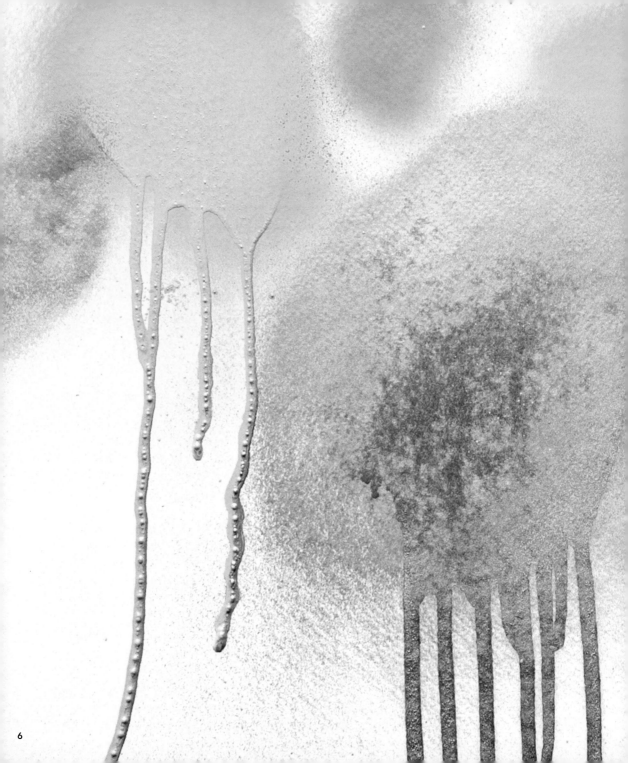

SPRAY

A spritz of color here and a dash of it there make everything look so much sweeter.

CHECKMATE CHESS JARS

→ **During my mother's first visit to Paris when she was 15,** a French chef and an African prime minister taught her how to play chess. Ever since then, the game has stuck—she was so excited when I was old enough to learn. Growing up with multiple boards in the house, a bishop or two were bound to go missing. When I didn't know what to do with an incomplete set, I found a way to give it a second life.

MATERIALS

Chess pieces

Spray paint

Strong glue

Jars

Newspaper

DIRECTIONS

► Remove lids from jars and place on sheet of newspaper

► Glue a chess piece to the center of the lid

► Once dry, spray-paint
Flip to the back of this book for a tutorial on how to spray-paint like a pro. It's easy, I swear.

► While lids dry, fill jars with candy, cookies, or anything else you like

STORY TIME

My mother's family chessboard was wrapped ten times over with masking tape. Every time my grandfather lost, he would break it in half and then apologize profusely. But it never stopped him from playing!

FARM-TO-TABLE BUTTER DISH

⟹ **If I'm using butter**, it's likely that whatever I'm putting it on is going to be eaten with my hands—which is why I find the lack of handles on most butter dishes so troubling. I decided to fix that. Now, the next time you eat that ear of corn or slice of toast, you won't have to struggle with slippery fingers and this no-handle nonsense.

MATERIALS

Glass butter dish

Small plastic farm animal toys (I found mine at KMart)

Spray paint

Strong glue

Newspaper

DIRECTIONS

► Set butter dish lid onto a sheet of newspaper

► Glue the toy to the center of the lid

► Once dry, apply spray paint to the lid

► Let dry before placing it on top of butter dish plate

TRY THIS!

Glue a few different animals onto the lid before applying spray paint for a herded handle.

GOLD PENCIL HOLDER

Writing utensils outnumber just about everything else in my room by roughly twenty to one. To keep them in one place, I upgraded a neglected ball of twine and found myself feeling even more inspired to write, sketch, and draw.

MATERIALS

Ball of twine

Spray paint

Newspaper

DIRECTIONS

▶ Place ball of twine on sheet of newspaper and apply gold spray paint

▶ Let dry

▶ Place pencils in the center of your golden ball of twine

QUOTE

"Let the world burn through you. Throw the prism light, white hot, on paper."
—RAY BRADBURY

STRIPED KITCHEN UTENSILS

I'm more likely to cook when whatever I'm holding makes me feel like Rachael Ray, which is why I showed these old salad utensils some love.

MATERIALS

Salad utensils

Spray paint

Fine-line masking tape

Newspaper

DIRECTIONS

▶ Cut 1-inch pieces of tape and wrap around utensil bases with a small space between each

▶ Wrap tape around the upper part of the handle to make sure paint doesn't land anywhere but on the handle

▶ Hold the utensil and apply spray paint

▶ Let dry by placing painted side up in a vase or jar

▶ Peel off tape

RECIPE

Take a break from making things beautiful and throw together a summer salad that my friends and I love:

SUMMER SALAD
1 cup orzo • ¾ cup toasted sliced almonds • handful of baby spinach • ¾ cup dried cranberries • 4 oz crumbled Gorgonzola cheese • salt and pepper — *Cook orzo, then stir into a bowl with sliced almonds, baby spinach, dried cranberries, and Gorgonzola cheese. Sprinkle on a little salt and pepper and enjoy!*

BOO BOTTLES

➡ **Bring recyclables back from the dead.** If you're looking for an alternative to a jack-o'-lantern or just don't feel like slicing your thumb open while making Halloween decorations this year, reclaim bottles from the bin and rejoice. Look for ones with interesting shapes—I chose Perrier bottles.

MATERIALS

Glass bottles

Spray paint

Permanent marker

Newspaper

DIRECTIONS

▶ Remove caps from bottles

▶ Place bottles on newspaper and apply white spray paint

▶ Use permanent marker to draw on oblong ovals for eyes and a mouth

TRY THIS!

Drop colorful straws into bottles and display on a table as party centerpieces.

EASY I.D. SERVING BOARD

➡ **Display different cheeses** or decode dried meats for your guests or detail your dinner menu right on your cutting board. If I'm not having guests over, I like to use mine as a leave-at-home shopping list or for reminders like: "Make that thing you've been dying to make for a week now!"

MATERIALS

Blackboard spray paint

Cutting board

Chalk

Newspaper

DIRECTIONS

▶ Place cutting board on sheet of newspaper

▶ Spray one side of cutting board with spray paint and let dry

▶ Cut charcuterie and cheese on the non-blackboard side—the knife can cut into the paint—and then flip over to lay out your spread

TIP!

Out of chalkboard paint? Make your own for under $5! Just mix one part nonsanded grout, which you can find at any home-goods store, with two parts latex paint in any color you like.

SWEETHEART SUGAR JAR

As a child, I had a sticker collection that I took far too seriously. Even though my book of Lisa Frank ponies and dogs is long gone, I still love an excuse to stick shapes on just about any surface. Read on for the grown-up's guide to stickers.

MATERIALS

Wire bale glass jar

Heart-shaped stickers

Spray paint

Newspaper

DIRECTIONS

▶ Evenly space stickers on the jar's surface

▶ Place jar on newspaper and coat with spray paint

▶ Let dry

▶ Peel stickers off and fill jar with sugar

TRY THIS!

For a polka dot jar, use circular price tag stickers you have lying around from your last yard sale and follow the steps above.

EASY OMBRE SCARF

Lavender looks good on everyone come spring and summer.

Here's how to brighten up your look with a few simple steps.

MATERIALS

Acid dye

Scarf

Hanger

Spray bottle

DIRECTIONS

▶ Follow the directions to prepare dye bath

▶ Pour dye into spray bottle

▶ Fold scarf over bottom rung of hanger and hang outside on a clothesline

▶ Hold spray bottle a foot away from fabric and begin spraying a foot above the bottom of the scarf

▶ Spray down to the edges of the scarf, moving the spray bottle closer to the fabric as you approach the ends—this will make the color on the bottom look darker

▶ Let dry

TIP!

Remember to add white vinegar to your dye! It makes every color come out brighter.

CUT & HANG

Get your scissors ready for quickie crafts that require only
a step or two but will leave you smiling for days.

FRAMED SCARVES

➡️ **Prettily patterned scarves** shouldn't be banished to a box under the bed as soon as the weather warms up. Here's how to store the winter staple and score a new piece of art all at once.

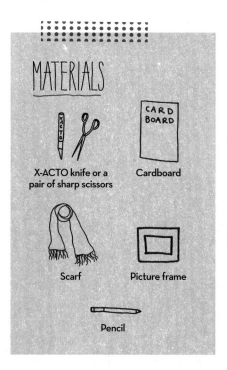

MATERIALS

X-ACTO knife or a pair of sharp scissors

Cardboard

CARD BOARD

Scarf

Picture frame

Pencil

DIRECTIONS

▶ Measure the size of your frame and mark off dimensions with a pencil on cardboard

▶ Use X-ACTO knife or scissors to cut cardboard to match dimensions

▶ Fold the scarf over the cardboard and pop into the frame. If there is extra scarf coming out of the back, just flatten it out as much as possible before replacing frame backing

▶ Hang

TIP!

For a cool art collection, frame multiple sheer scarves with striped and floral prints and hang together on a wall.

SNEAKY HOLIDAY STORAGE

"Just because Christmas is over doesn't mean I'm ready to pack up the garland," said me every year since I was ten. Rather than tucking decorations into a box and stashing them in the closet, I found a fun way to display holiday shimmer all year long. Stow gold décor this way, and when the holidays come back around, take decorations out to hang.

MATERIALS

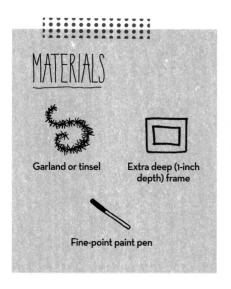

Garland or tinsel

Extra deep (1-inch depth) frame

Fine-point paint pen

DIRECTIONS

▶ Write a message on the front of the frame glass with the paint pen

▶ Open the frame and pile in garland, tinsel or both

▶ Close frame and hang

TRY THIS!

Got small Christmas ornaments? Use double-sided tape to secure glass baubles to a piece of white paper and place in a frame for year-round glittery globes.

Presenting
SAN Rose Cinemas
BEASTS OF THE SOUTHE
4:40pm Sun 8/5/2012
ADULTS $12.00

Barely Jade™

Seashells

S

Seashells suggest the delight taken by the
sickly Paul Dombey in contemplating the ocean
with his sister, Florence, in *Dombey and Son*:

*"Sister and brother wound their arms around
each other, and the gold light came streaming in,
and fell upon them, locked together. How fast
the river runs ...! But it's very near the sea. I hear
the waves!" Presently he told her that the motion
of the boat upon the stream was lulling him to
rest. How green the banks were now, how bright
the flowers growing on them, and how tall the
rushes! Now the boat was out at sea, but gliding
smoothly on. And now there was a shore
before him. Who stood on the bank?"*
—From *Dombey and Son*, ch. 16

Charles Dickens, *The Key to Character* at The New York Public Library.
Not intended for sale

CLIP-ON PHOTO COLLAGE

➡ **It's fun to think outside the frame.** Give it a try.

MATERIALS

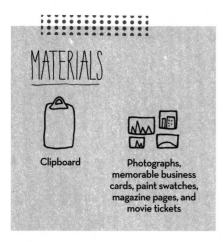

Clipboard

Photographs, memorable business cards, paint swatches, magazine pages, and movie tickets

DIRECTIONS

▶ Clip photographs, magazine pages, and everything else onto a clipboard

▶ Hang

STORY TIME

My favorite photograph of all time captures my grandfather embracing my grandmother under Brooklyn's Coney Island pier when they were going steady (they started dating when she was 12 and he was 13!).

STOCKING FLOWERPOT

⟹ **Instead of tossing torn or ripped tights**, try this two-second technique to give small pots some texture.

MATERIALS

Scissors

Tights

Flowerpot

DIRECTIONS

▶ Cut the foot plus some extra off of a pair of tights

▶ Pull the foot onto flowerpot

TIP!

To water the thick-leaved echeveria succulent seen here, fill a spray bottle with water and spritz the soil.

WOODEN PHONE CASE

Make your phone look like it could fit in with the forest. (No trees were harmed in the making of this craft.)

MATERIALS

Wood grain contact paper

Scissors

Pencil

Phone case

DIRECTIONS

▶ Roll out contact paper so that the lined inside is facing upward

▶ Trace around phone case on paper—and remember to trace the oval cutout for the camera, too!

▶ Cut out the traced shape with scissors

▶ Peel contact paper from paper backing and stick onto phone case

TRY THIS!

Any kind of contact paper can work here, so don't be afraid to choose your favorite.

SAN JUAN
FORT

BIRTHDAY
VACAY

EMILY
IN NYC

COOKIE CUTTER FRAMES

➡️ **When I'm not baking cookies,** I'm figuring out ways to put my most adorable confectionary cutters to work. The result: a new way to display photographs.

MATERIALS

Pencil

Scissors

Cookie cutters

Photos

DIRECTIONS

▶ Place cookie cutter on top of photo

▶ Trace outer edge of cookie cutter

▶ Cut photograph along traced edge

▶ Pop into the back of cookie cutter

TIP!

If photos don't fit perfectly into your cookie cutters, apply strips of washi tape (patterned Japanese tape—you can find it on Etsy or at Target) around the edges to secure the photo in its newfound frame.

MEMORY WRAPPING PAPER

I love the feeling of friction when you pull free a piece of twine or the slick slip of a silky bow between your fingers. Sometimes, the experience of opening a present is just as valuable as the gift itself. Make your rip, tug, and tear mean something more with your all-time favorite photos right at your fingertips.

MATERIALS

Photos

Paper

Tape

Photocopier

DIRECTIONS

▶ Tape photos onto a sheet of paper and photocopy

▶ Wrap present with photocopied paper

STORY TIME

To wrap these small boxes, I photocopied pictures from my family's trip to Barcelona, Spain. Every year for Christmas, we opt out of gift giving to travel to a new place together and explore.

PENCIL VASE

Brighten up a bouquet with colored pencils. Just do it. (Can Nike sue me for that? No? Just checking!)

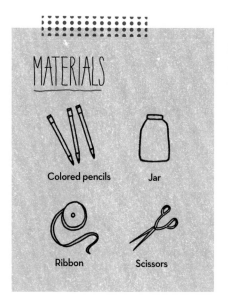

MATERIALS

Colored pencils

Jar

Ribbon

Scissors

DIRECTIONS

▶ Hold colored pencils against the outside of a jar

▶ Cut piece of ribbon and tie around pencils to keep them in place

QUOTE

"And so our mothers and grandmothers have, more often than not anonymously, handed on the creative spark, the seed of the flower they themselves never hoped to see—or like a sealed letter they could not plainly read."
—ALICE WALKER

WRITE & PAINT

There's no need for an art degree here. If you can splash, smudge, and scribble, then we're all set.

PERSONALIZED TEAPOT

Sometimes things are not as easy as they look. This is not one of those things. Draw whatever you like onto your favorite pot and read on to learn how to make it stick.

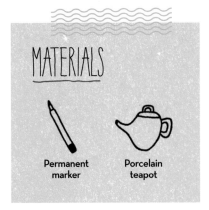

MATERIALS

Permanent marker

Porcelain teapot

DIRECTIONS

▶ Draw design onto teapot with a permanent marker

▶ Place in oven at 350° Fahrenheit for 30 minutes

▶ Remove, let cool, and start steeping

TRY THIS!

More for color than black and white? Opt for permanent markers in bright shades.

MESSAGE STONES

Here it goes... Roses are red,
Stones are free,
Poems are hard,
Stones

MATERIALS

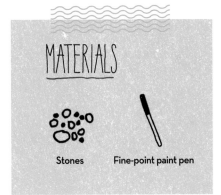

Stones   Fine-point paint pen

DIRECTIONS

► Clean off stones with water and let dry

► Write words or phrases on stones with paint pen

STORY TIME

A lot of time and thought went into deciding what to write on those rocks. Just kidding! After a burger, a pickle back, and a brief discussion about this craft, a friend of mine blurted out, "Peace, love... whatever." What can I say? She's a genius.

SPELL-OUT SPICE JARS

⟹ **Keep your spices straight**—and learn how to cook something new, too!

MATERIALS

Jars

Fine-point paint pen

Paper

Printer

Scissors

Tape

DIRECTIONS

▶ Type out the name of an herb or spice in your favorite font

▶ Print

▶ Cut out the word

▶ Slip inside the jar and tape to the glass

▶ Trace the letters with the paint pen

▶ Remove slip of paper and fill jar with spices

RECIPE

Some people shoot in studios, others shoot wherever they can find good light and—in my case—great food. While snapping away with photographer Meera Lee in her family's home, I was pulled aside by Meera's mother, who taught me about Indian food and flavors. Her spice secrets to the perfect curry: turmeric and chili powder, cumin, mustard seeds, and salt.

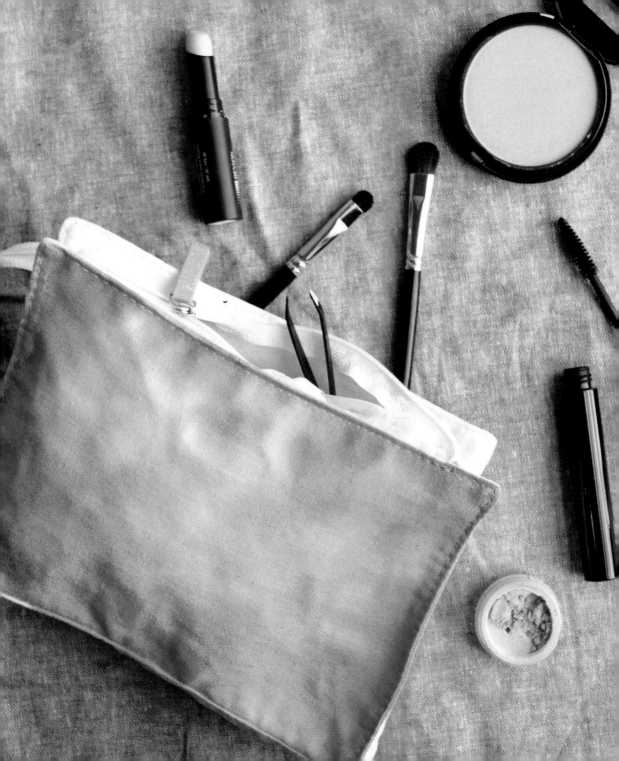

NO-TIE TIE-DYE MAKEUP BAG

⟹ **In life, there are long ways and there are shortcuts.** Long ways build character. Shortcuts get you a bright makeup bag in minutes. Here, a way to cheat tie-dyeing by using markers and a first aid essential:

MATERIALS

Canvas makeup bag

Colored markers

Rubbing alcohol

Paper towel

DIRECTIONS

▶ Use markers to draw patches of color onto makeup bag

▶ Pour rubbing alcohol onto paper towel

▶ Smudge wet paper towel on makeup bag to blur colors

▶ Let dry

TIP!
Try this craft in the sink to minimize the mess.

TAKEOUT LANTERNS

Order in and score mood lighting for more dinners to come.

MATERIALS

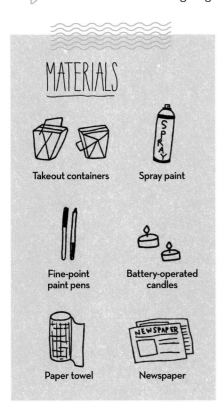

Takeout containers

Spray paint

Fine-point paint pens

Battery-operated candles

Paper towel

Newspaper

DIRECTIONS

▶ Clean takeout containers with wet paper towel and place on a sheet of newspaper

▶ Apply spray paint to containers and let dry or keep them their original color

▶ Draw banners, sayings, or patterns onto container sides with paint pen

▶ Drop in battery-operated candle and close container top

TIP!

Ask the restaurant you're ordering from to throw in an extra takeout container. They usually don't mind and that way you can make sure your lantern looks like new.

SPLASHED PAINT VOTIVES

➡ **I don't mind finding beauty in the mess of things.** Which is why, after a stare-down with one very lucky cup of dirty paint water, I splashed color on just about everything within my reach.

MATERIALS

Acrylic paints

Paintbrush

Glass votives

DIRECTIONS

► Dip brush into paint and then into a cup of water

► Scribble brush on the inside of votive—try not to overlap scribbles so colors don't blend into brown

TIP!

Try listening to "Bloom" by The Paper Kites while crafting your votives.

MOBY-DICK

GREAT SHORT WORKS OF Henry James

SIGNAL CLASSIC CQ 599 The Sketch Book Washington Irving 451-CQ599-175

T. SCOTT FITZGERALD Tender Is the Night SCRIBNERS

Treasure Island Robert Louis Stevenson PENGUIN CLASSICS

FAVORITE POEMS OF EMILY DICKINSON AVENEL

LOLITA

BRICK BOOKENDS

Books hide out like dust bunnies in my apartment. Whenever I think they're all on the bookshelf, I find one under the bed and another in a forgotten tote bag—I swear they have minds of their own. To group your precious reads together, camouflage old bricks and use them as sneaky props to keep wild reads from getting away from you.

MATERIALS

Two bricks

Acrylic paints

Fine-point paint pens

DIRECTIONS

▶ Wash bricks with water

▶ Once dry, coat one edge with acrylic paint

▶ Use paint pen to write out book title

▶ Let dry

TIP!

The more battered the brick, the better! Nicks and bumps supply a great textured canvas for the paint and make for vintage-looking spines.

FADE-AWAY ROLLING PIN

Half of the reason I like to bake cookies is that I get an excuse to pull this rolling pin out of the drawer. The other half is that I have the most ridiculous sweet tooth ever. The next time you find yourself waiting for gingersnaps to cook through, give handles a pick-me-up in under a minute.

MATERIALS

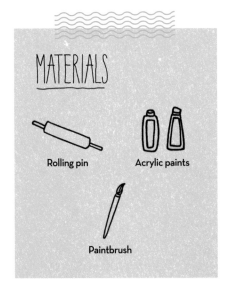

Rolling pin

Acrylic paints

Paintbrush

DIRECTIONS

▶ Start at the base of the rolling pin handle and apply progressively darker paint as you brush your way up the handle

TIP!

If your handle starts to look striped instead of faded, wet your brush and blend between the two colors.

FAUX FRENCH LOCKETS

Glossy, colorful French lockets are perfect in every way, except for the fact that they cost $100. Follow these steps and make your own for pennies.

MATERIALS

An old locket   Colored nail polish

DIRECTIONS

▶ Apply a layer of nail polish to the face of an old locket and let dry

TRY THIS!

Add small stones and beads (I strung a flower charm onto one of mine) to personalize your pendant.

COLOR-ME THUMBTACKS

➡️ **Make something of your message board** with thumbtacks as cool as the ideas you pin up.

MATERIALS

Thumbtacks   Nail polish

DIRECTIONS

▶ Hold the pin end of the thumbtack in your hand

▶ Paint the top with nail polish and let dry

▶ Push them through a piece of paper or cardstock to store them together

LISTEN

Play Alt-J's "Breezeblocks"... and "Matilda"...and "Tessellate." Actually, just listen to all of Alt-J.

COLOR BLOCK LOCK

Yes, I'm that person in your way at the gym because she forgot which locker she put her sneakers in. Sorry! Here is how to spot your locked-up stuff from across the room.

MATERIALS

Nail polish   Combination lock

DIRECTIONS

▶ Apply nail polish to the arm of a combination lock in thick stripes

▶ Let dry

TRY THIS!

Into sports? Paint your lock in your favorite team's colors to show some spirit.

MAP MAKEOVER

⇨ **Whenever I am overwhelmed by a case of wanderlust**, I unfold a map and plot out my next adventure. To keep my inspiration feeling fresh, I decided to put a tattered classic of the U.S. to good use.

MATERIALS

Map

3-inch vinyl letters (the cling-on, window decoration kind available at art stores)

Acrylic paint in white

Paintbrush

DIRECTIONS

▶ Unfold map and lay on a flat surface

▶ Place letters on map to spell out a phrase

▶ Coat entire map with white paint

▶ Once dry, peel letters off of map

LISTEN

Play "Atlas Hands" by Benjamin Francis Leftwich and just try not to book a flight.

PAINTED PILLOWS

➡ **Perfect for a rainy afternoon or a night in**. Draw out a pattern (even visit your favorite online shop and copy one of theirs), and then it's the simple matter of staying within the lines.

MATERIALS

Acrylic paints

Paintbrush

White pillow or pillowcase

Pencil

DIRECTIONS

▶ Draw out pattern design in pencil on pillow or pillow cases

▶ Trace over and color in pattern with paint

▶ Let dry

TIP!

You don't need to be an artist to make them: keep patterns simple by sticking with scallop shapes and small plus signs.

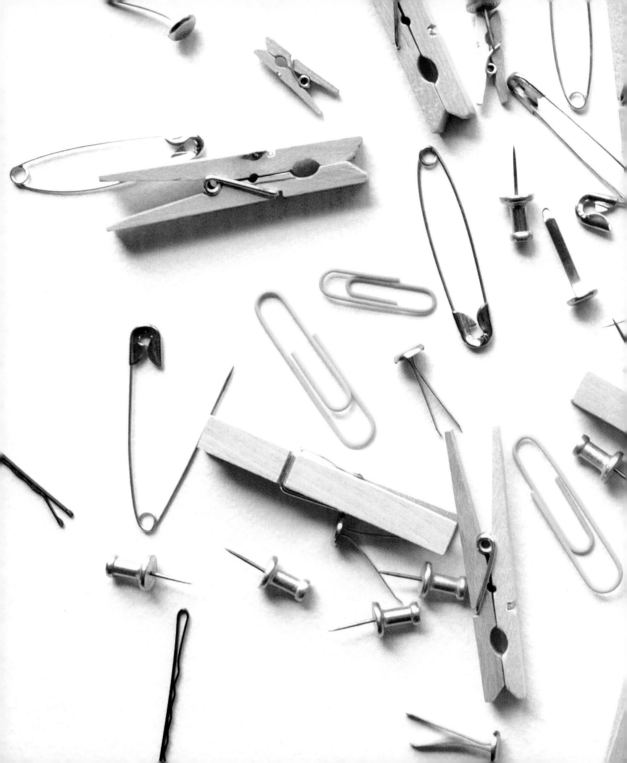

PIN & FOLD

Bobby pins, paper clips, and napkins get new names with a few simple sleight-of-hand tricks.

PAPERCLIP SKEWERS

➥ **Let's dissect the word toothpick, shall we?** A device to "pick" at one's "tooth." I don't know about you, but that doesn't sound appetizing to me. The next time you entertain, try this easy origami trick for the everyday office supply and leave the wooden sticks for their true intention.

MATERIALS

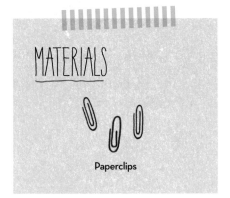

Paperclips

DIRECTIONS

▶ Bend back the paperclip's longest outer wire in half to make a V shape

▶ Bend the inner smaller stretch of wire outward so that the edge of the heart touches the elongated piece of wire

▶ Skewer fruit

TRY THIS!

Works great as a cupcake topper, too!

73

CELEBRATION NAPKIN BANNER

Sometimes you need to celebrate for absolutely no reason at all. It's the first official day of winter? Don a party hat. Today is Tuesday? Break out the noisemakers. You're wearing a white shirt? Hooray for you! If there's no champagne to pop, put your napkins to some greater than good use.

MATERIALS

Colorful paper napkins

Twine

Solid brass fasteners

Scissors

DIRECTIONS

► Cut twine for however long you want your banner to be

► Fold napkin in half diagonally over twine

► Push brass fastener through napkin under the twine

► Repeat

STORY TIME

We photographed this banner on the brick wall of my apartment building. After taking a few shots, we decided to leave it hanging up. The next morning, I caught people posing under it for pictures!

BOBBY PIN BURST COASTERS

➡️ **When I worked at a beauty magazine**, bobby pins permanently littered my desk like confetti on post-parade New York City streets. Before long, inspiration set in and the crafts just kept coming.

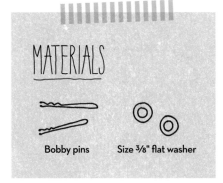

MATERIALS

Bobby pins

Size ⅜" flat washer

DIRECTIONS

▶ Slip bobby pins onto washer with the prongs pointed outward

▶ Continue around the whole circumference of the washer

LISTEN

Turn up "Ceilings" by Local Natives and relax while threading pins onto washers.

TRINKET TEA TAGS

After living in London for a year, I became quite the tea drinker. As my friends can attest, tea of the bagged, loose leaf, and flower varieties has become a staple in my apartment. In short: those closest to me have also been converted to loving it, too. Here is a fun project for a tea party or a quick solution for too many steeping cups on the kitchen counter.

MATERIALS

Large safety pins

Bits of string, charms from old necklaces, beads, bows, and just about anything else that tickles your fancy

DIRECTIONS

▶ Tie string, slide beads, or hook an old charm onto safety pins to tell beverages apart

TRY THIS!

These work great on wine glasses, too. With a little extra push, you can even poke them through the handles of plastic cutlery to keep down the waste at a party.

PAINT-SWATCH KEY HOOKS

Leave your key ring on a table and it falls off, place it in a pocket and you'll forget which one, throw it in your bag and it'll hide out for hours. To truly keep tabs on keys, place them here and you won't have to think about them a minute more.

MATERIALS

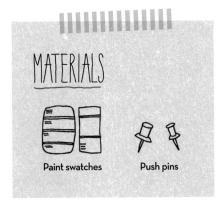

Paint swatches   Push pins

DIRECTIONS

▶ Arrange paint swatches on the wall and secure them with push pins

▶ Hang keys from push pins

TRY THIS!

Looking to change up the color palette in your living room or hallway? Perfect. Swap out pinned paint swatches for new ones to highlight the new shade scheme.

Lincoln Center

MAKERS: Women Who Make America Premiere
Proudly Presented By
AOL, PBS & Simple Facial Skincare

Wed, February 06, 2013 7:00 pm
Alice Tully Hall, Starr Theater, Broadway at 65th Street

STUFF

MARY THULL
● ● ●

Dear AJ,

Hello dearie! I hope you're all well in New York! Paris is amazing, but I miss you guys! I'm having a bit of a hard time doing something that's... I might do something happy for a bit due to my inability to find a job (oh, poor me, ha ha) but I'll still be in London in April! I'll try to get you guys some Cadbury, but I can't promise I won't eat it before I next see you! If you have any requests from Paris, though, just let me know! (Oh, also, you would love the fashion, trends here, everyone is so effortlessly...)

Bisous!
Anna ♡

A'
145 Soccer
New York, NY 10005
USA

THINKING OF YOU

INSPIRATION CLOTHESLINE

Growing up in Brooklyn, New York, I used to love looking out my bedroom window during the summer months at colorful T-shirts and underwear hung up to dry and zig-zagging down the block like the world's longest banner. There's always been a place in my heart for clotheslines, especially when they can make you smile and keep you feeling creative. Here is how to make one on your bedroom or office wall.

MATERIALS

Twine

Scissors

Small screw eyes

Clothespins

DIRECTIONS

▶ Insert screw eyes into the wall about a foot or so apart from one another

▶ Cut your desired length of twine (I keep mine around 2 yards for a larger wall)

▶ Use twine to tie a knot to the first screw eye

▶ Thread twine through remaining hooks

▶ Use twine to tie a knot to the last hook

▶ Use clothespins to hang magazine tear-outs, memorable birthdays cards, and just about anything else

STORY TIME

The inspiration clothesline was one of the first crafts I created—and I like to think that it inspired me to get into more DIY stuff.

Whether it comes in strips or dollops, sticky stuff can upgrade picture frames, revamp notebooks, and reinvent holiday décor.

TAPE & GLUE

LITTLE LINED FRAMES

➡ **If frames start to chip or scuff,** give them a fresh start. It's seriously too easy.

MATERIALS

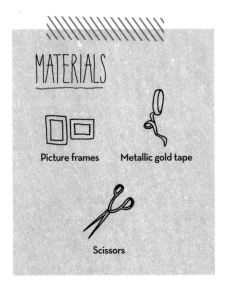

Picture frames

Metallic gold tape

Scissors

DIRECTIONS

▶ Cut 1-inch strips of metallic gold tape

▶ Wrap tape around frame sides or corners

▶ Hang

TIP!

Got mismatched frames? Good. Gold accents make wooden, white, circular, and square varieties feel like they're all in the family.

TIC TAC SPICE RACK TO GO

→ **Try packing for a weekend away** with a small duffle bag and *lots* of shoes. Spices are expensive and I wasn't willing to give them up and be left cooking perfectly bland chicken in my favorite flats. My solution? Reinventing the classic dispenser, which yielded a bunch of positives like well-spiced chicken marinara, extra space in my luggage, and really fresh breath.

MATERIALS

5 boxes of Tic Tacs

Double-sided tape

Spices

Washi tape

Nail polish remover

DIRECTIONS

▶ Peel off labels from Tic Tac boxes, wiping away the label glue with nail polish remover

▶ Wash thoroughly and let dry

▶ Cut double-sided tape into 1-inch strips and adhere to the sides of boxes. Push box sides against each other to make them stick together

▶ Fill with spices—I used salt, powdered garlic, ground ginger, a salt and pepper mixture, and pepper for an ombre effect

▶ Line top and bottom with washi tape for added color

TRY THIS!

I roll a piece of paper into a funnel and pour seasonings through it. That way I don't end up with a curried countertop.

89

PANTONE PLACEMAT

⇨ **Create a color scheme that inspires you.** Lay it on the table. Have your hue and eat off of it, too.

MATERIALS

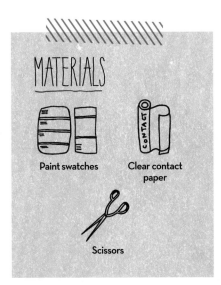

Paint swatches

Clear contact paper

Scissors

DIRECTIONS

▶ Cut a rectangular sheet of contact paper

▶ Peel contact paper from the adhesive backing and lay sticky side up, taping the corners to your workstation surface

▶ Arrange and overlap paint swatches on the contact paper

▶ Apply a second layer of contact paper on top of the paint swatches—press along the surface to eliminate air bubbles

▶ Pull the placemat free from the tape and use scissors to cut around the paint swatches

LISTEN

Play "All I Want" by Kodaline while creating this craft. It's just oh-so perfect.

with my mind
on
my writing
and
my writing
on my mind

i'm not a
poet i just
rhyme a lot

WRAPPED NOTEBOOKS

➡ **It's as simple as it sounds.** Notebooks. Wrapped. Done. To try a quirkier version (and a throwback to second-grade grammar), try making up beats and rhymes for this project's homophone variation.

MATERIALS

Fine-point paint pen

Notebook

Metallic tape

Washi tape

DIRECTIONS

▶ Wrap tape along and around notebook covers, or get creative with your favorite rhymes

TRY THIS!

Once you get started thinking of literary approaches to rap songs, you won't be able to stop. For example: "I like big books and I cannot lie!" and "Writing it and writing it and writing it well."

TRAVELING GLOBE

I love to collect items from my travels, but sometimes I'm not quite sure what to do with them once I return home. A figurine of Barcelona's La Sagrada Família, a mini-statue of London's Big Ben, a tiny-town version of the Arc de Triomphe—they wind up cluttering my desk and then ultimately crowding my drawers. That's why I thought they deserved some extra TLC.

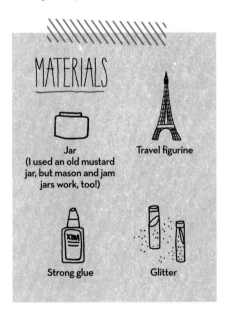

MATERIALS

Jar
(I used an old mustard jar, but mason and jam jars work, too!)

Travel figurine

Strong glue

Glitter

DIRECTIONS

▶ Remove lid from jar

▶ Glue base of figurine to inside of lid

▶ Once glue is dry, fill jar to the brim with water and shake in glitter

▶ Screw lid back onto jar

▶ Shake and enjoy

TIP!

If glitter looks clumpy at first, don't fret. Give the sparkles a day or two to settle in the globe.

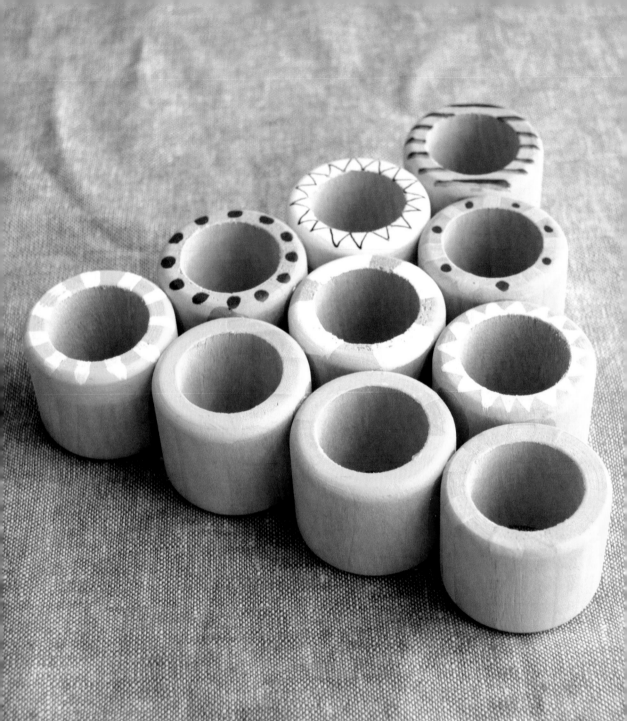

RETRO RECYCLED TRIVET

After uncovering a bin of old wooden napkin rings at a flea market in Brooklyn, I decided that a little paint and some super-strong glue would be enough to turn nothing special into something different.

MATERIALS

Strong glue

Wooden napkin rings

Acrylic paints

Paintbrush

Wax paper

DIRECTIONS

▶ Paint lip of napkin ring with geometric shapes

▶ Once paint dries, place napkin rings on wax paper (unlike newspaper, glue won't stick to wax paper) in a triangular shape

▶ Apply glue to one side of napkin ring and press against another napkin ring

▶ Repeat until rings are glued together in a triangle shape

▶ Let dry

TRY THIS!

Have different sets of napkin rings that have been hibernating? Perfect. Mix up rings and glue together in a triangle, square, or hexagon for a quirky, geometric trivet.

CANDY HAIR TIES

➡ **Stop yourself from eating mountains** of those message-bearing Sweetheart candies around Valentine's Day by turning them into accessories. Look at that! A new incentive to cut down on the sweets.

MATERIALS

Acrylic paints

Paintbrush

Sweetheart candies

Clear top coat nail polish

Thick-band hair ties

Strong glue

DIRECTIONS

▶ Apply a coat of clear nail polish to Sweetheart candies

▶ Once dry, paint entire candy with gold paint

▶ Apply glue to one side of candy and press against hair tie

▶ Let dry

TRY THIS!

You can also use circular Red Hots or squares of Chiclets gum.

BRIGHT LIGHT ORNAMENTS

When a bulb dies, give it a better fate than whatever the trash can has to offer.

MATERIALS

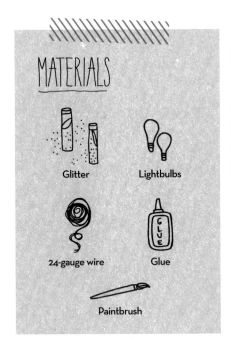

Glitter

Lightbulbs

24-gauge wire

Glue

Paintbrush

DIRECTIONS

► Use paintbrush to cover bulb with glue

► Sprinkle glitter onto bulb

► Wrap wire around neck of bulb five times and tie, leaving 1 inch of wire remaining

► Knot the ends of the wires to create a loop

► Hang

TIP!

Finding the perfect bulb for this craft is kind of like cloud gazing: look past the object's function and just try to see the shape. Round appliance bulbs and icicle-shaped, candelabra-base incandescent variations make for interesting tree decorations.

STRING NAPKIN RINGS

➡ **It's the night before your housewarming** and you're looking for a quick décor fix that feels fresh (and will impress guests). Here is an effortless way to make the place settings look a little sweeter when you don't have a minute to waste.

MATERIALS

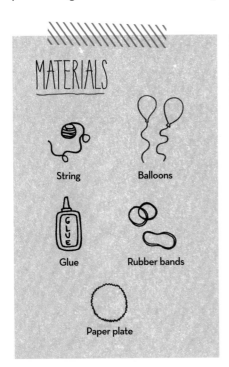

String

Balloons

Glue

Rubber bands

Paper plate

DIRECTIONS

▶ Blow up a balloon until it reaches the size of a kiwi or large lemon and secure with a rubber band so the air doesn't escape

▶ Pour glue onto a paper plate

▶ Cut about 16 inches of string and roll the strand in the glue, coating it all the way around

▶ Wrap string around the middle of the balloon

▶ Once completely dry, remove rubber band and pull out the deflated balloon

▶ Pull napkins through your new napkin rings and place on the table

TRY IT!
Use ribbon instead of string for a thick-banded ring.

TIME CAPSULE TERRARIUM

If you're sentimental like me, odds are you may have a few of your favorite childhood toys lying around—or, most likely, hidden in a drawer. Here's how to turn them into something worthy of being on display.

MATERIALS

Small figurines

Moss

Pebbles

Glass terrarium jar— or any jar will do

Strong glue

DIRECTIONS

▶ Glue figurine to a small, flat stone

▶ Remove jar lid and fill terrarium with a layer of pebbles and top with moss

▶ Place figurine-topped pebble on top of moss

▶ Replace lid

TRY THIS!

Add Lego figures to your terrarium for a fun twist on the whimsical world.

DIP & STAMP

Blueberry-dyed
stationery and pencil-
stamped boxes? You will
never look at plain paper the
same way again.

BERRY STATIONERY

➡️ **Have some old blueberries left over in the fridge?** Perfect. Let's make something of them, shall we?

MATERIALS

1 cup of blueberries

3 cups of water

Cardstock

Pot

DIRECTIONS

▶ Pour 3 cups of water into a small pot and heat over a high flame for 15 minutes

▶ Stir and smash blueberries to extract a strong color

▶ Dip cardstock into dyed water

▶ Let cardstock dry

TIP!

To let stationery dry without disturbing the dye, secure the cardstock to a wire hanger with clothespins.

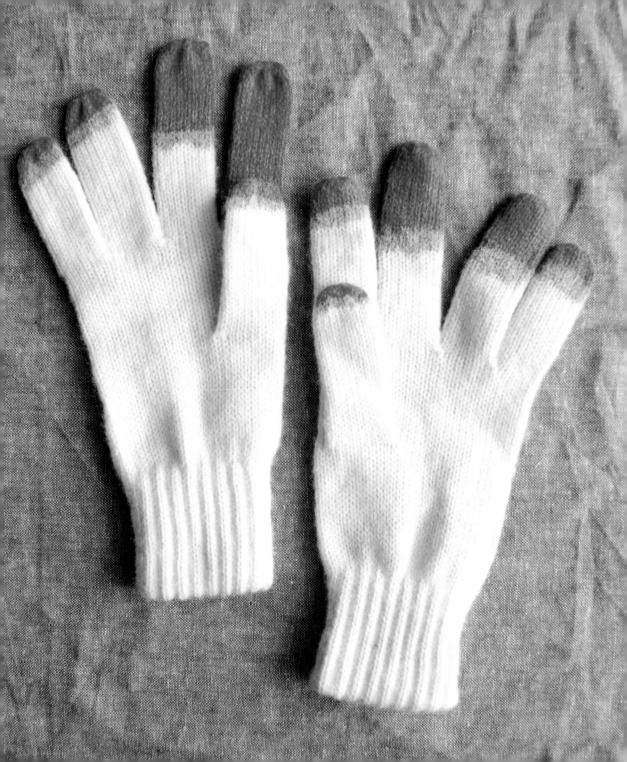

DIP-DYED GLOVES

➡️ **Two-tone winter essentials** are trendy and fun to make.

MATERIALS

White gloves   Acid dye

Pot

DIRECTIONS

- ► Follow the directions to prepare a dye bath
- ► Dip glove fingers one at a time into dye bath, holding each dyed tip away from the glove so as not to spread color to the remaining white parts
- ► Let dry

STORY TIME

Do you see how the pink color fades into the white on each finger? Fancy, right? Not at all. You can't prevent it from happening, actually, as the dye will bleed a little bit into the pristine part of the glove. The result: less work and you look like a pro.

CHOCOLATE JEWELRY BOX

⇨ **After scarfing down a box of chocolates on Valentine's Day,** I decided to get creative with Russell Stover. Here's how to turn a chocolate box into a heart that holds rings and just about anything else you need it to.

MATERIALS

Heart-shaped chocolate box

Acrylic paints

Spray paint

Pencil

Newspaper

DIRECTIONS

▶ Remove lid from heart box and place top side up beside box on newspaper

▶ Apply spray paint to the box's lid and sides

▶ Once dry, dip pencil eraser into pink paint and press polka dots onto box lid

▶ Let dry

QUOTE

"There is nothing better than a friend, unless it is a friend with chocolate."
—LINDA GRAYSON

COLOR CLOTHESPIN MIRROR

➡ **Pinch these paint-tipped pins** onto a small reflective surface and perk up wall decorations stat.

MATERIALS

Wooden clothespins

Acrylic paints

Paper cup

Small mirror

DIRECTIONS

▶ Pour acrylic paint into cup

▶ Dip clothespin ends into the paint

▶ Hang clothespins on a clothesline until dry

▶ Pin around a mirror's perimeter

TRY THIS!

Maybe you don't have a mirror lying around, but you did find a plate at a yard sale that's just too cute to eat off of. Try this project out and turn dinnerware into décor.

PATTERNED ENVELOPES

➡ **"Snail mail is dead," they said.** "Just give up," they said. But e-mails don't crinkle and yellow with time the way letters do. Therefore, I refuse to let go. May you always make time to send a card—and I hope this easy trick makes each one look even more special than the last.

MATERIALS

Envelopes

Stamps

INK

Ink pad

DIRECTIONS

▶ Stamp the inner lip of envelopes

TRY THIS!

Whenever I send a letter, I drop a sprig of rosemary or thyme into the envelope for some added herbal notes.

POLKA DOT NAPKIN

➡️ **Do you have one minute?** Good. Make it matter.

MATERIALS

Wine cork

Acrylic paints

Cloth napkin

DIRECTIONS

▶ Dip wine cork top into paint

▶ Press onto napkin

▶ Repeat

QUOTE

"...a polka dot has the form of the sun, which is a symbol of the energy of the whole world and our living life, and also the form of the moon, which is calm. Round, soft, colorful, senseless and unknowing. Polka dots become movement... Polka dots are a way to infinity."
—YAYOI KUSAMA

SPAGHETTI-STAMPED TOTE BAG

⟹ **Growing up, I could always expect to find the smell of sauce** instead of scented candles upon passing through my family's front door. Sundays meant pasta; Mondays, school and then pasta. And Tuesday: leftover pasta. Here is the result of a lifetime of playing with food when I wasn't supposed to and having far too much access to every kind of spaghetti and ravioli ever made.

MATERIALS

Rigatoni pasta **Canvas tote**

Acrylic paints

DIRECTIONS

▶ Smooth out tote bag on a flat surface

▶ Dip one open end of a rigatoni into acrylic paint

▶ Press onto tote

▶ Repeat in any pattern you like

TIP!

Rigatoni isn't the only pasta perfect for stamping! Turn to the stamp guide on page 124 to find out which other Italian specialty made the list.

SPRAY DAY

Everything you need to know about spray-painting, I've jotted down right here. Follow these ten tips and get started—you might not be able to stop.

1

PICK YOUR PRIMER
Use a gray primer before applying dark-colored spray paints. For pastel colors, opt for a matte white primer.

2

KNOW YOUR BRAND
My favorite spray paint brand is Ironlak—which offers so many beautiful colors like the peachy "Volcano" and powdery blue "Atmosphere" hues used for the Checkmate Chess Jars (page 8)—but hardware store-bought Krylon works, too!

3

SET IN THE SUN
Place your spray-painted items out in the sun to cut the dry time in half.

7

TEST IT
Before applying to your project, spray a bit of paint on a piece of newspaper to make sure everything is coming out smoothly.

4

BOX THEM UP
To avoid getting spray paint all over yourself on a windy day, arrange your objects inside a box before spraying. If you're spraying a lot of small objects, lay them down next to each other and spray all at once.

8

GO SIDE TO SIDE
Spray from side to side in sweeping motions, holding the can about 6 to 8 inches away from the object, for complete color.

5

WIPE AWAY DUST
Go over the object with a rag right before spray-painting to prevent a speckled color.

9

LESS IS MORE
Multiple thin coats of paint are better than one thick layer. Spray a fine mist all over your project. If you notice an area that needs more paint, wait 10 minutes for the project to dry and then go at it again.

10

STORE SMARTLY
Spray-paint valves can get clogged if they are not used for a while. To prevent this, hold the can upside down and spray for 5 seconds before putting on the cap and storing.

6

SHAKE IT
Really! Shake the can for at least 30 seconds for the smoothest application possible.

ONE-SECOND STAMPS

They've been in the fruit basket, bouquet, and side table drawer the whole time. Here are lots of free impressions you can find around the house—all you need is some paint.

BELL PEPPER
Slice off the top of a pepper and use the stem as a handle.

COTTON SWAB
Perfect for small polka dots.

ROTELLE PASTA
Add this detailed shape to your décor using a paintbrush and a little paint.

LEMON
A simple way to make the perfect mandala.

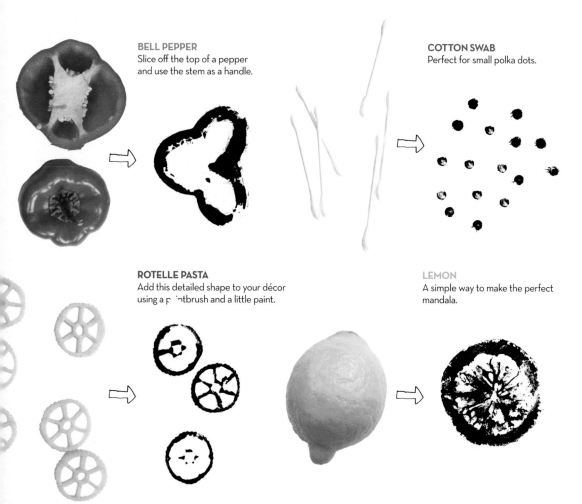

STRAWBERRY
Cut strawberries in half, dip into paint, and stamp—don't forget to add a small stem and seeds with acrylic paint.

FLOWER
Watch buds bloom into firework patterns on paper.

CELERY
Opt for watercolor paint with this stamp for sweet, transparent curls.

LIGHTER
Who knew the bottom of a lighter could make this retro print?

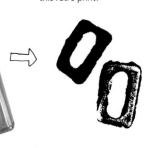

MUSHROOM
Remove the stem and add paint to the cap's rim before pressing.

YOGURT-COVERED PRETZELS
Got a few stale snacks lying around? Use them to create this sweetheart print.

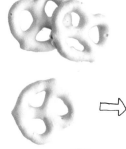

INDEX

✳ ✳ ✳

Alison Caporimo is writer with a penchant for crafts, reading, tea, and talking about London (where she lived for a short while). A native New Yorker, Alison found her inspiration for style and design while blogging and going on coffee runs for *Harper's Bazaar*. Her work has appeared in magazines like *Allure* and *Every Day with Rachael Ray*, and she is currently the senior associate editor at *Reader's Digest* magazine, covering the topics of home décor, financial advice, popular culture and travel. She lives in a Brooklyn apartment with more terrariums than you can handle.

Meera Lee Patel is an artist raised by the New Jersey shore, where she swam the bright waters and climbed cherry blossom trees until she grew old enough to draw them. Her illustrations, inspired by the magical mysteries of nature, have appeared in publications such as *Organic Gardening* and *Jamie Magazine* and have been translated into housewares and apparel by Free People, Poketo, and Urban Outfitters. In addition to illustration and photography, she produces her own line of stationary and textile products. Meera lives in and works from her studio in Jersey City, New Jersey. Visit her at www.meeralee.com.

ACKNOWLEDGMENTS

For the family, friends, and colleagues that have supported me along the way, I owe this project to you. To my parents, James and Marie, you two are the inspiration behind everything I create. Thank you for the endless love and encouragement—I can't imagine being any luckier. To my sister, Lauren, thank you for always being my biggest cheerleader. I attribute my love affair with crafting to the memories of Vincent and Nancy Fraumeni and Josephine Caporimo, who always knew how to use their hands. As for my writing, I owe it all to Vincent Caporimo, who taught me how to tell a story. To my friends, thank you for your faith, motivation, and the tea breaks—my dear friends Stephen, Kiera, and Chesler for the late-night brainstorms and the occasional (though much needed) glass of wine.

A sincere thank you to my editor, Katherine Furman, who believed in this project from the start and met with me over chai lattes (and sometimes a pickle back) to keep me feeling inspired. I could not have made this book without you. To the amazing team at Ulysses Press—your excitement was contagious and kept me going at 3AM, gluing together odds and ends that would, hopefully, transmogrify into something beautiful. To Elliot Stokes, for his amazing eye and beautiful designs. To my wonderful photographer and illustrator, Meera Patel—this book is as much mine as it is yours. Thank you for the great company at 5AM photo shoots on snowy days so we could get the lighting just right and for the passion you threw into this project. Also, I'd like to thank the Patel family, who opened their doors (literally) to the effort that was this book.

Finally, to Liz Vacariello, Courtenay Smith, and the amazing staff at *Reader's Digest*. You have been so supportive throughout this process and it has truly meant so much. To Linda Wells and the wonderful teams I've had the honor of working with at *Harper's Bazaar, Allure,* and *Every Day with Rachael Ray*. Thank you to my first magazine hero, Maura Kutner, who had faith in me long before this journey began, and those to follow: Mark Singer, Elizabeth Angell, Kristin Perrotta, and Sonal Dutt. A huge thank you to my dear friend Sarah Wexler, who has counseled me every step of the way and inspired me in my writing and beyond. Also, I must thank the small seed of a school that grew into Bay Ridge Prep—the place where I first learned to think outside the box. All my love.